Rebuilding **lives**

images in the aftermath

To the people and communities who have endured so much and shared their extraordinary stories of survival and hope.

Title: Rebuilding lives: images in the aftermath

ISBN: 978-0-646-50800-9

Subjects: Natural disasters
Emergency relief
Poverty

World Vision Australia
1 Vision Drive
Burwood East Victoria 3151

Design: Justin Dymott
Words: Lisa Hodson
Images: Rebecca Murray
Editing: Justin Dymott, Lisa Hodson, Rebecca Murray
Production: Virginia Gissara
Liaison: Kam Shafaati
Project management: Amy Chemay, Anna Gigliotti, Lani Masuku

Printed by Whirlwind Print

World Vision Australia ABN 28 004 778 081 is a Christian relief, development and advocacy organisation dedicated to working with children, families and communities to overcome poverty and injustice.

Contents

Rebuilding **lives**

images in the aftermath

Foreword

Cyclone. Earthquake. Flood. Famine.

When a natural disaster hits, the shock is instant. The need is immediate and basic: food, shelter, water, medicines. When the people affected are already battling poverty, resources can be scarce, making relief efforts that much harder.

It's difficult work for emergency teams in a humanitarian disaster, heartbreaking at times. But for World Vision it remains a privilege to be invited into a community that wishes to begin anew; to be asked to work with people who want to rebuild their lives.

With so much turmoil in our world, both natural and man-made, there are many recent examples of this - Myanmar's deadly Cyclone Nargis and China's tragic earthquake of 2008; the devastating food crisis currently gripping the developing world. In the immediate aftermath of the 2004 Asian Tsunami, I witnessed firsthand people's courage and determination to rebuild - truly the best and the worst of times.

The worst of times: in Sri Lanka, seeing things that no human should have to suffer. The power of a wave; a wave of death that snatched hundreds of thousands of lives; a wave of grief for those left behind; a wave of utter destruction of lives, homes and of hopes.

And the best of times: the experience of coming back to Australia and seeing a wave of compassion, a wave of generosity, a wave of solidarity with people in their pain. In my lifetime, I have not seen anything like it.

Messages of solidarity don't bring back lives, but they do promise hope. As witnesses to the pain of people devastated by the tsunami and too many other emergencies since, World Vision continues to partner with generous Australians, assisting survivors to keep going, to rebuild and re-skill and re-establish, in whatever ways they can.

Here then are the stories of some of the millions of people we have stood beside. If you have ever contributed to a World Vision emergency appeal, they have benefited in many ways from your assistance, and from your insistence that this moment of time should not remain their worst of times – but a new beginning.

Tim Costello
World Vision Australia Chief Executive

Rebuilding **lives**

images in the aftermath

Introduction

The Global Rapid Response Team, a group of 28 highly trained technical experts, is capable of arriving at the scene of an emergency within 48 hours, providing immediate assistance in areas as diverse as water and sanitation engineering, humanitarian protection, food relief, shelter and health. In addition, we have response teams in each of the regions to provide further surge capacity, and we are continually training our 25,000 national staff across the world in effective rapid response.

The events of December 2004, when the Asian Tsunami devastated coastal populations, represented a watershed moment in the way World Vision responds to emergencies. The enormous global effort by the organisation to promote recovery following this disaster also provided World Vision with a wealth of understanding on how to better assist communities responding to emergencies.

Since that time, regions affected by the tsunami have largely returned to normal, with economic circumstances in many cases improved from their pre-tsunami status. World Vision has gone on to use these learnings to respond more effectively to over 20 large-scale emergencies across Asia, Africa, Central and South America and the Pacific.

In the past four years World Vision has created a network of technical experts for crisis contexts which is truly global. None of this would have been possible without the generous support of our donors and sponsors. We are deeply grateful for the trust these individuals, governments and organisations place in World Vision, as we continue our work assisting communities across the world to recover from emergencies.

Graham Tardif
Head of Humanitarian & Emergency Affairs
World Vision Australia

Earthquake

Iran

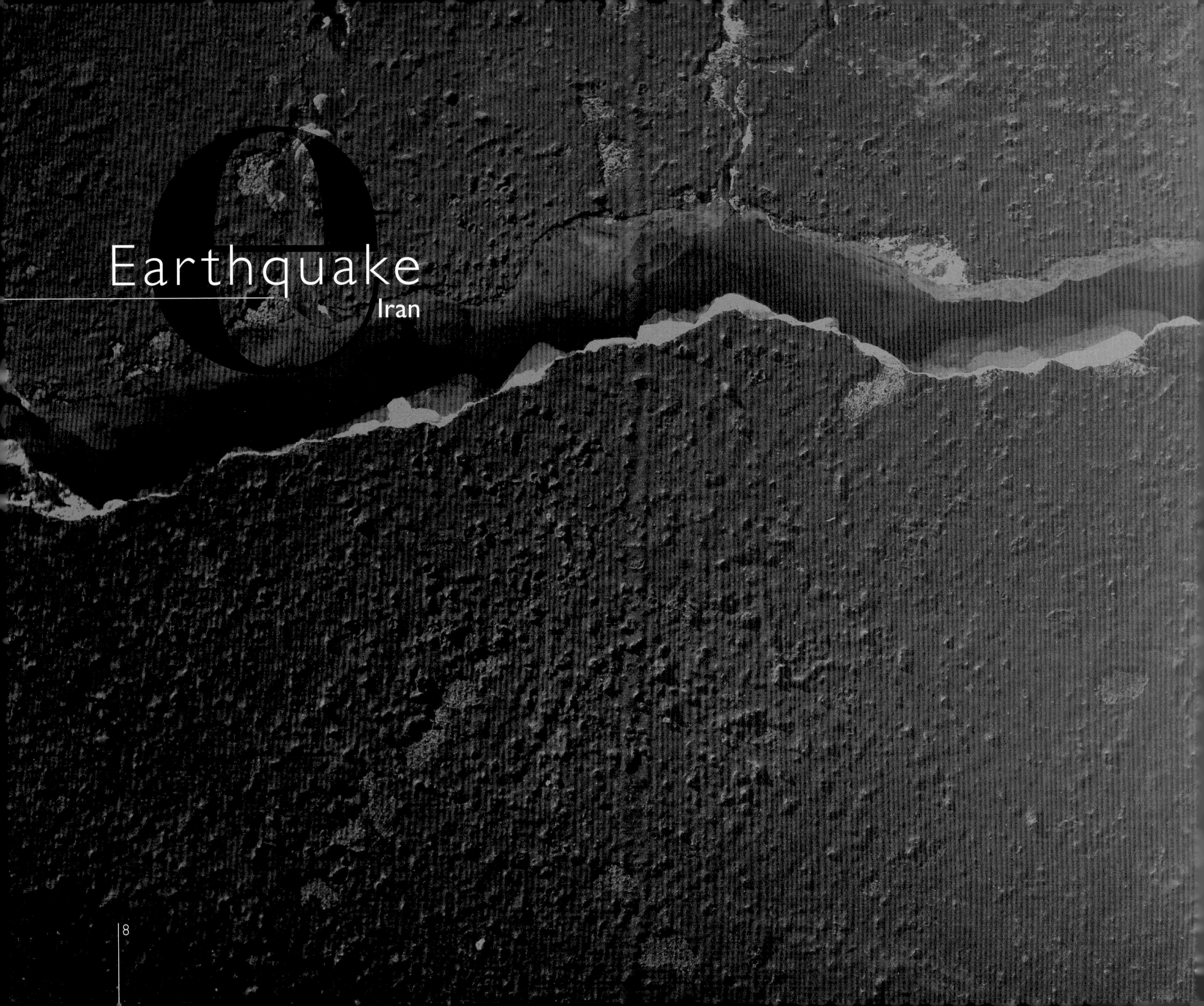

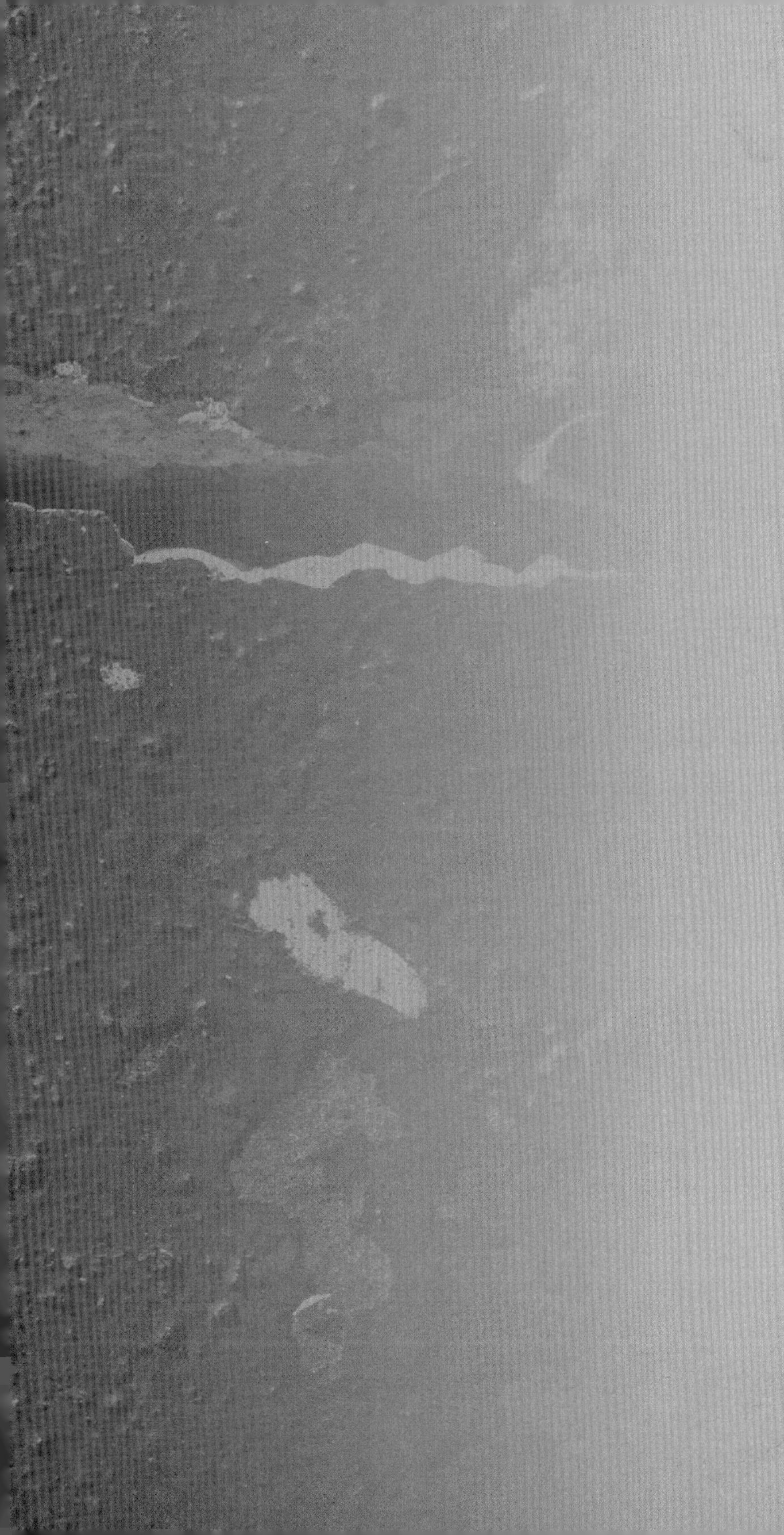

Earthquake

Iran

The historic city of Bam, located in southeast Iran, was devastated by a major earthquake at approximately 5:30 am on 26 December 2003. Officials estimate well over 26,000 people were killed and approximately 40,000 people injured.

The majority of the city's buildings, mostly constructed from mud brick, clay and straw, collapsed, leaving tens of thousands of people buried. Most of the homes left standing sustained serious structural damage and were too dangerous to even enter. An estimated 90 percent of Bam's medical facilities were destroyed by the quake. Education, health and sanitation services were severely impaired.

World Vision began work in Bam within 48 hours of the earthquake. Partnering with national organisations such as the Iranian Red Crescent Society, World Vision distributed tents, tarpaulins and other emergency items, such as blankets, kitchen kits, stoves, shoes, hygiene kits and jerry cans.

Staff then turned their attention to the many schools, health centres and houses that needed to be restored or rebuilt. World Vision's relief program helped more than 50,000 people directly, and thousands more indirectly, with the re-establishment of essential services. Australian contributions created three new health centres, designed to withstand regular seismic activity in the area. These health centres now provide basic healthcare, dental services and child health and nutrition services for up to 60,000 families in the Bam province each year.

e

Earthquake
Iran

Roya, 11, lost her cousin, uncle and aunt in the earthquake.

"I loved my aunt as much as the world. I don't know what to do to lessen my pain."

Earthquake
Iran

Only the steel door of this home in Bam city's District 3 remained standing following the earthquake.

Earthquake
Iran

Mohammad Ali Tajik, holding his only surviving child, Zahra, aged 4. Zahra lost her two sisters aged 5 and 7, and her brother, aged 9, in the disaster.

Earthquake
Iran

Standing in the ruins of their living room, Hossein Ali Chel Tokhmi and his wife talk through an interpreter to Greg Campbell from World Vision's Global Rapid Response Team.

Earthquake
Iran

A string of tents line a street in Bam. People displaced by the earthquake often set up shelter just metres from the ruins of their former homes.

Earthquake
Iran

Abbas, 7, was 175 kilometres away when the quake struck. He returned to the news that his mother's sister had died in the disaster. "I lost my aunt and I'm sad. I loved her very much."

His mother said, "We adults don't understand life and these things. How can a child understand it?"

Earthquake
Iran

Following a World Vision distribution, Fatemeh and her daughter wheel home tools and a hygiene kit. Fatemeh's entire family was affected by the disaster: losing friends and extended family, as well as the loss of material belongings and a sense of safety.

"My mother pulled me from the ruins and took me to the hospital. I can't sleep at night now. I'm frightened, especially when there are aftershocks," said Fatemeh's elder daughter.

World Vision

Earthquake
Iran

Ali, 10, lost a cousin and his father was injured in the disaster. Here he poses with a pick axe, part of a tool kit supplied to survivors by World Vision and the Iranian Red Crescent Society. After struggling for days, many people said they were grateful for tools that allowed them to retrieve household goods from beneath the rubble.

"It was an experiment," said World Vision's Paul Sitnam. "The goals were twofold, the practical and the psycho-social; tools to dig out essential items and a simple way of giving hope, by providing a means to start putting people's lives back together on the most basic level."

Earthquake
Iran

Mehdi (standing with his back to the camera) moved his wife and 7-month-old daughter into a tent next to the rubble of their home after the earthquake hit. World Vision staff, assessing rebuilding needs in the neighbourhood, discovered that not only did Mehdi need a new latrine, but he could build them too! Mehdi managed to rescue welding equipment - his main tool of trade - from the debris. With his cousins and little nephew lending a hand, Mehdi and World Vision set out to help others in the district, building emergency latrines and bathing cubicles.

e

Earthquake

Iran

"This tent is a place of joy and life in contrast to the rubble and debris outside. I'm so glad (it's) possible for children to begin to return to normality through activities like this."
– Dave Robinson, World Vision

Before World Vision and local partners set up Child Friendly Spaces like this tent, the children of Bam would pass the day unsupervised, roaming through collapsed buildings, at dire risk of injury from debris on the ground and falling bricks from above.

Earthquake
Iran

A table set up in front of a Bam guest house displays photos of people from the neighbourhood who died in the earthquake. People dropped by photos, flowers and memorabilia to be displayed on the makeshift memorial. A banner above the table read: 'Bam Is Still Alive.'

"As long as there is life there is hope. Humanity is strong. It is my duty to stay here and help build up the town."
– Akbar Panjali Zadeh, guest house owner

Tsunami

Asia

Tsunami

Asia

On the morning of 26 December 2004, a massive undersea earthquake off the west coast of Indonesia triggered a series of tsunami waves that crashed across the Indian Ocean. Coastlines in a dozen countries were affected and more than 225,000 people are believed to have died. The scale of the destruction was both shocking and previously unimaginable to many people.

An unprecedented outpouring of support from a stunned global community saw World Vision mount its largest-ever single relief response simultaneously across Indonesia, Sri Lanka, Thailand and India. After community consultation, the restoration of basic services and the supply of survival items like food, water, shelter and medicines became the agency's first priority, followed by the construction of infrastructure – homes, schools, bridges, roads and canals. World Vision established more than 200 Child Friendly Spaces to support the emotional and physical safety needs of orphaned and traumatised children, and provided employment training and educational opportunities for thousands of survivors.

World Vision's largest relief response in history came to a close at the end of December 2007, and affected communities are now steering their own futures. World Vision continues to fund long-term community development programs throughout Indonesia, Sri Lanka, India, Thailand and Myanmar, and also funds emergency relief projects in conflict-affected areas of Sri Lanka.

Tsunami
Asia

Everyday items in the rubble underscore the devastation wrought on so many people's lives by the tsunami.

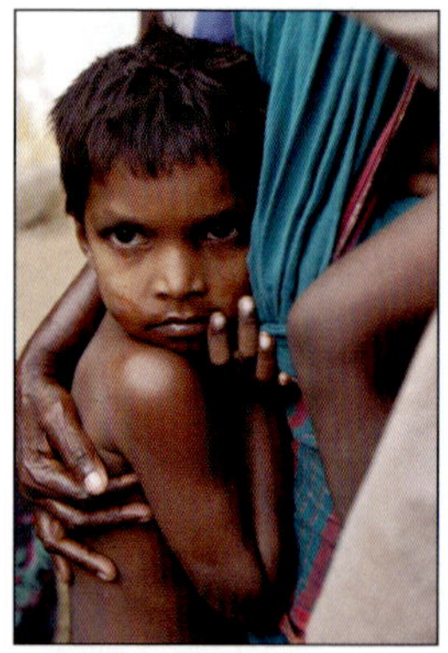

Kathirvan, 5, clings to his mother while waiting to be immunised. His family survived the wave, but their home and possessions were all washed away.

Tsunami
Asia

Fisherman Chandrasegar purchased the newest boat in his fleet just weeks before the tsunami. He saw older boats float to safety, while his hit the trees.

t

Tsunami
Asia

The needs of people affected by the tsunami went beyond mere survival. World Vision makes it a priority to also care for the psychological impacts these disasters have on communities, individuals and especially, children.

"We need to restore hope, especially for the children."
– Sherine Kara, World Vision

t

Tsunami
Asia

Viramuthu keeps a vigil on the beach, mourning the loss of his wife Shanthini.

t

Tsunami
Asia

Karupayee lost nine relatives in the tsunami, including her husband and two granddaughters. Karupayee's husband was holding on to a coconut tree alongside her awaiting rescue when he was swept away.

Tsunami
Asia

Scenes of devastation in Banda Aceh, as people struggle to recover their lives amid the rubble.

t

Tsunami
Asia

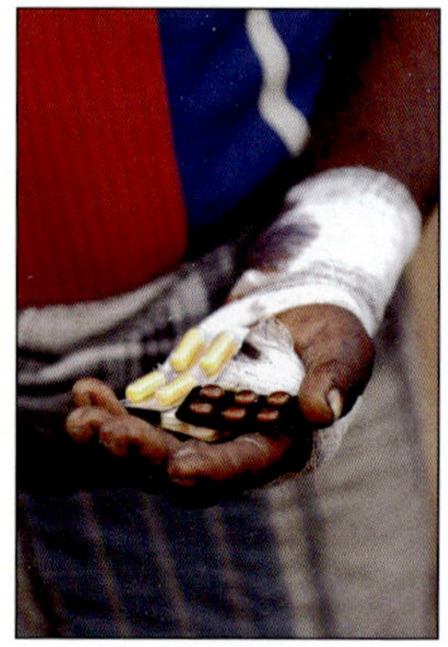

Fisherman Sinaathambi receives antibiotics for the wounds he suffered, after being thrown into trees and buildings and dragged through torn bushes by the tsunami waves.

"I don't know how I managed to escape that day. I don't know how I can look at the sea again. After I am cured from this injury, there is no way I will go back on the sea."

Tsunami
Asia

Stacking water bottles in a Sumatran warehouse used by World Vision to store relief supplies.

OZON
AIR MINUM DALAM KEMASAN
ALUMINIUM PRODUCTS
MASPION GROUP

t

Tsunami
Asia

World Vision distributed emergency relief supplies to more than 27,500 people displaced along the coast south of Colombo, Sri Lanka.

World Vision

Tsunami
Asia

Unprecedented international cooperation among governments, international aid agencies and community groups saw the swift distribution of relief to 12 affected countries.

P.T. GAPURA ANGKASA
NRG-5
World Vision
World Vision

t

Tsunami
Asia

The best assistance for "children affected by the tsunami is to help them return to their normal lives by providing them with the security, educational needs and nutrition they need."
– World Vision's Chandila Colombege

Tsunami
Asia

Families and vulnerable children needed a roof over their heads while World Vision worked over the longer term to help provide people with permanent homes. A number of housing options made available to displaced people helped ease hardship for many families in this part of Colombo.

Tsunami
Asia

Almost 200 children have a safe, comfortable learning environment after a new school and kindergarten was built by World Vision. The tsunami killed many students and completely destroyed the original buildings, leaving only their foundations.

"Many children have been traumatised by the conflict and the tsunami but, at this kindergarten, they are able to share and study together again," said kindergarten principal Harnanunsa Emma Mutya.

The new village of Saney, Banda Aceh, constructed by World Vision.

Back in business: fishermen bring their day's catch to the port.

Tsunami
Asia

Boats handed over to fishermen in Lhoong, Aceh. The boats helped more than 65 fishermen from four villages.

01

Tsunami
Asia

Two weeks after the tsunami: the destroyed village of Keudah in Banda Aceh.

Two years after the tsunami: World Vision housing construction projects have transformed Keudah.

Earthquake
Pakistan

Earthquake

Pakistan

A massive earthquake struck northern Pakistan on 8 October 2005, killing 75,000 people and leaving 3 million more homeless.

World Vision provided urgently-needed relief supplies such as winter-ready tents, blankets, food and water. Staff worked with local agencies to distribute hygiene and sanitary items, and provided medical kits and tools to affected families.

Relief efforts were hampered by the onset of the harsh Pakistani winter. Heavy rain and snow restricted helicopter access, and landslides blocked many key roads into the mountainous area. World Vision Chief Executive, Tim Costello, observed: "While Australians bask in our summer, severe weather conditions in Pakistan are exacerbating the plight of those who have already lost so much."

As the immediate needs of those affected were met, World Vision continued to support families living in the region by working on resettlement and rehabilitation. Education, child protection and livelihood issues became the focus of programs which continue today.

Earthquake
Pakistan

A man holding a young child walks along the edge of a collapsed roadway.

(FWO)

Earthquake
Pakistan

No one could walk down these streets until rubble tossed by the earthquake was cleared.

Earthquake
Pakistan

A woman waits to receive her food ration at World Vision's distribution point in Jabouri, in Pakistan's North West Frontier Province.

Men kneel to pray in the shadow of a destroyed building.

Earthquake
Pakistan

Children carrying heavy water containers from a mountain spring, situated an hour's walk from their home in Jhangi village.

Asma (pictured front) was in school when the earthquake killed her mother and brother, crushed all 45 houses in Jhangi and destroyed the village's water system.

e

Earthquake
Pakistan

An elderly Pashtun man pauses on a mountain trail above the Siran Valley, in Pakistan's North West Frontier Province. The Pashtun people and their antecedents have lived in Afghanistan and northern Pakistan since around the time of Alexander the Great, three centuries before the birth of Christ. They have a reputation as fierce warriors and fiercely traditional Muslims.

Earthquake
Pakistan

Emergency shelter equipment is among the essential items being unloaded from this truck for the 260 families of Pettekka village.

Earthquake
Pakistan

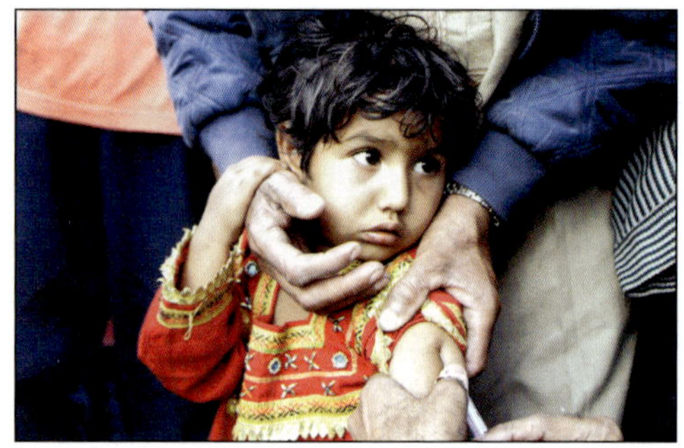

A young girl is immunised to protect her against the potential outbreak of disease in the disaster's aftermath.

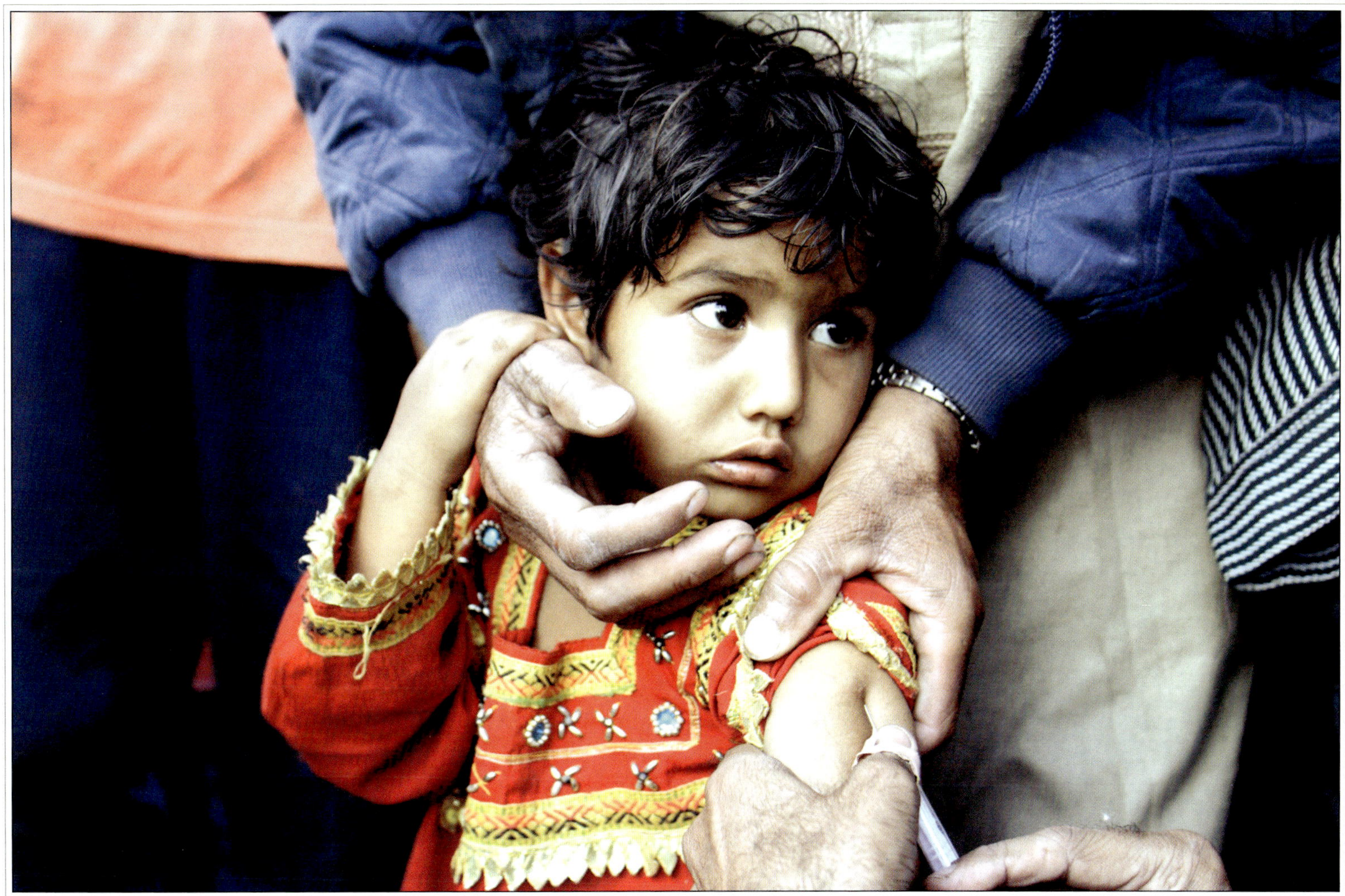

Earthquake
Pakistan

Mohammud Shafee with son Anisur aged 7, at World Vision's distribution point in Jabouri. Mohammud collected a hygiene kit for his family, which included a blanket and knitted clothing supplied by Australian donors.

ABC

Children at a Child Friendly Space in Khori village in the North West Frontier Province.

World Visi
Aktion
Deutschland Hilft
CHILD FRIENDLY SPACE
(بچوں کی تربیت گاہ)

Earthquake
Pakistan

A community elder in Kotkay village in northwestern Pakistan talks to World Vision's Farid Alam.

Farid reported: "Their needs are tremendous, but so is their will to improve their children's lives."

Earthquake
Pakistan

These women, newly skilled tailors and embroiderers, are graduates of World Vision's six week cutting and stitching course in the Siran Valley. Some of these students had previously owned sewing machines, but the precious tools were destroyed in the earthquake. With their certificates and new sewing machines, the group now plan to create opportunities to increase their family incomes. Participant Gul Nisa, whose house and family shop was destroyed in the earthquake: "Now I can make nice clothes for my family. I hope to earn some money too, when I stitch clothes for other people."

SALIKA
MODEL
NO:
COLOUR
DATE
MANUFACTURERS
SALIKA SEWING MACHINE CO.(PVT) LTD.

Primary school students at Dhabar Katta village. The original school was destroyed during the earthquake, leaving its 135 students from grades one to five in a temporary building with only one teacher.

Earthquake
Pakistan

Villagers work quickly to level concrete across this much-needed access road to their village. Roads throughout the Siran Valley were devastated by the earthquake, shattering infrastructure and people's livelihoods. World Vision projects to widen roads, improve surfacing and reconstruct access roads have benefited around 3,300 households.

"We have had great difficulties moving down the sick and infirm people to main Siran Valley road for onwards travelling to hospital. We also had a great problem going to the water mill for grinding wheat flour, going to market and coming back with a heavy load of household goods," said Mohammad Iqbal, a mason who worked on the construction. "This road will make access to market easy."

Cyclone
Myanmar

Cyclone

Myanmar

In the late afternoon of 2 May 2008, a strong wind started blowing across the Ayeyarwady Delta of Myanmar. Within a few hours, sea water started rising and the winds became ferocious.

Cyclone Nargis hit the low-lying areas of south-western Myanmar that night. Official figures state almost 140,000 people were killed or reported missing. One of the greatest impacts of the disaster was the destruction of livelihoods across the hard-hit Ayeyarwady Delta and Yangon. Some 2 million livestock were lost to the storm, a million acres of rice paddy inundated with salt water, and hundreds of fishing vessels and critical infrastructure wiped out.

Since the cyclone hit, World Vision has been part of the international relief response to support the 2.4 million people who were severely affected. Emergency supplies such as food, medicines, safe drinking water and shelter equipment were despatched. Ground staff worked with emergency teams to set up protection programs including Child Friendly Spaces.

In addition to child protection, World Vision's ongoing rehabilitation response includes assisting communities with water, sanitation and hygiene programs, and the re-establishment of fishing and farming industries.

Cyclone
Myanmar

On 2 May, Nway aged 7, left her family's little bamboo and wooden house in the Ayeyarwady Delta to stay with her aunt and uncle. Within a few hours, what seemed a brewing thunderstorm became much more destructive. Sea water started rising and Nway fled with her aunt and uncle to the house of the village head for safety. "It was totally dark but very noisy. We fell into the water several times. Water came into my mouth."

More than 100 villagers crowded into the house and stood together, praying for the storm to end. Water was now up to three metres deep outside. Shortly after midnight the wind stopped, but nobody dared go outside. Injured and frightened, they waited for the dawn.

When the sun came up, the village head's house was the only one still standing. Survivors searched but only recovered dead bodies under the debris. A quarter of the population of 400 perished, most of them women and children. Among them were Nway's parents and her three siblings. Nway took shelter with others at a nearby village, where she received food and clothing, including her favourite, a yellow silk blouse.

Cyclone
Myanmar

"Children are among the most vulnerable after a disaster like Cyclone Nargis and require special attention to see them through the hard times that follow."
– Judy Moore, World Vision

Cyclone
Myanmar

Rubble and debris being cleared with any available tools before reconstruction can begin.

C

Cyclone
Myanmar

When the storm surge from Cyclone Nargis hit, Koko held his little sister (pictured) whilst he clung to a palm tree. The rest of his family were swept away and lost.

Cyclone
Myanmar

Emergency shelter kits, designed locally and distributed by World Vision, are offloaded from a helicopter during the relief operation. In many of the villages in the cyclone-affected delta, more than 80 percent of the buildings sustained heavy damage. The kits, containing tarpaulins and bamboo poles, were distributed to almost 57,000 households.

WFP
UR - 25514

Cyclone
Myanmar

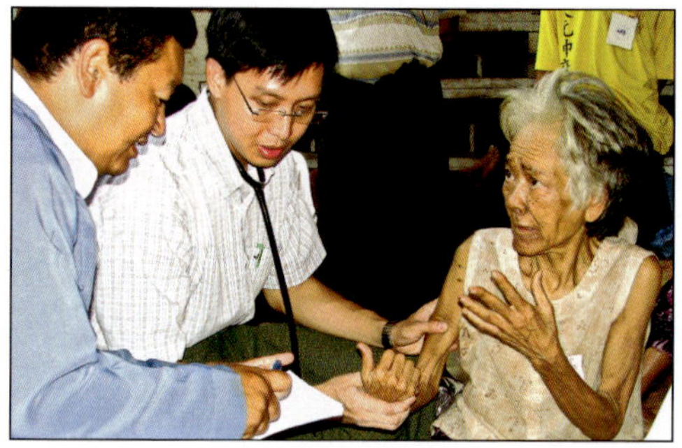

Mobile health clinics are set up in the days immediately after an emergency to replace damaged hospitals and health centres. Trained medical staff provide first aid for survivors, monitor their ongoing health and wellbeing, and work to prevent the spread of disease.

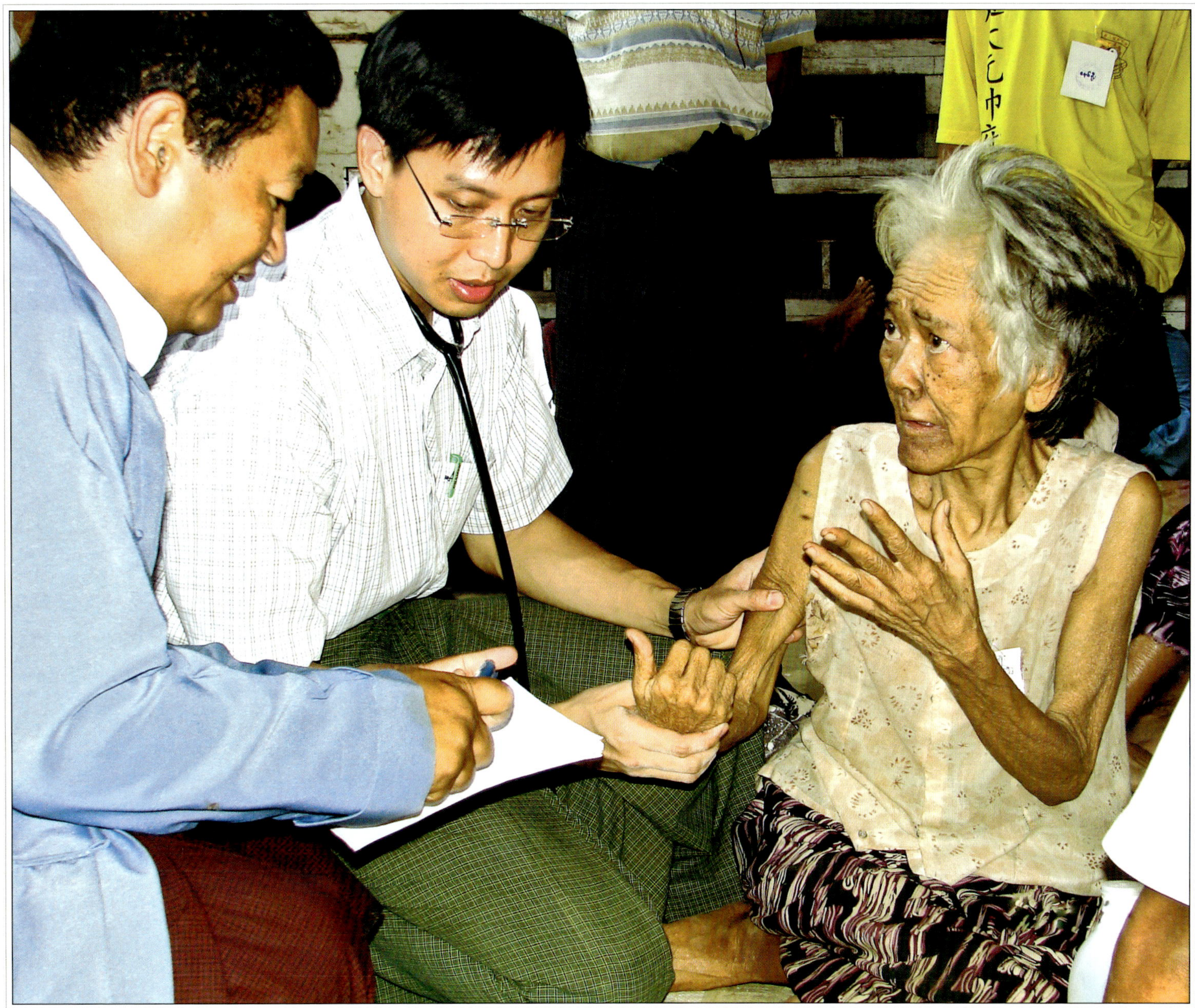

Cyclone
Myanmar

Some villages in the Ayeyarwady Delta were inaccessible after the cyclone. In this heavy-hit coastal area, a cart is being used to move shelter kits down the beach to the village.

Cyclone
Myanmar

Emergency food aid is distributed in Bogalay. Over 220,000 people received supplies of rice, oil and pulses in the first two weeks after the cyclone.

pean Commission
ogramme
WFP
WFP
Net Weight 50 kg
June 2008
ne 2008

Cyclone
Myanmar

Residents help distribute relief and reconstruction items in this delta village.

Cyclone
Myanmar

"I feel really happy as I could let him drink this clean water."

This mother was very concerned about giving her son dirty rainwater, after her village's water pond was contaminated with debris and saltwater in the storm. World Vision has helped communities clean up more than 250 water ponds in the delta; a water purification unit is now providing clean drinking water for this village.

Cyclone
Myanmar

A farmer in the cyclone-hit delta on Heingyi Island is ploughing his field in early August, weeks later than the regular planting season. Many fields were inundated with salt water when Cyclone Nargis struck, leaving them too contaminated with salt to grow rice well. This farmer hopes to salvage something from the harvest to feed his family.

Cyclone
Myanmar

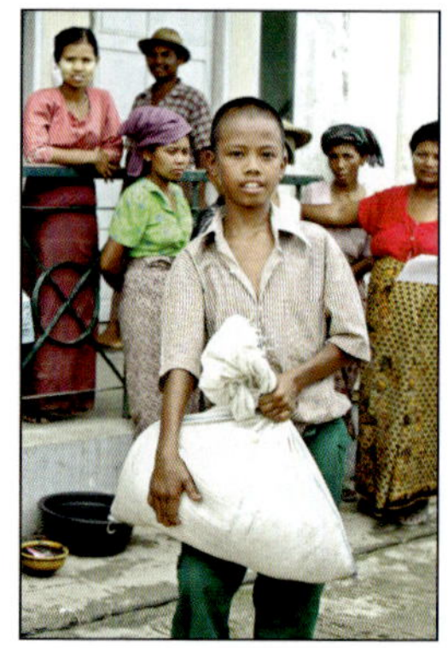

In the wake of the cyclone, Aung has taken on the responsibility of providing food for his family and doesn't have time to play with his friends. "But I'm happy to receive the rice for my family."

"With the economic impact of Nargis hitting many families hard, children risk having to take up work and contribute to the family's income, rather than remaining in the classroom to learn and grow."
– Makiba Yamano, World Vision

Cyclone
Myanmar

Children gather in the riverside village of Bogalay. Up to half the children from this village were killed in the cyclone.

After disasters, children are at greater risk of abuse, violence, exploitation and neglect. Child Friendly Spaces can provide critical support for the protection and recovery of these children, and ongoing encouragement for school-aged children to continue their education.

Earthquake
China

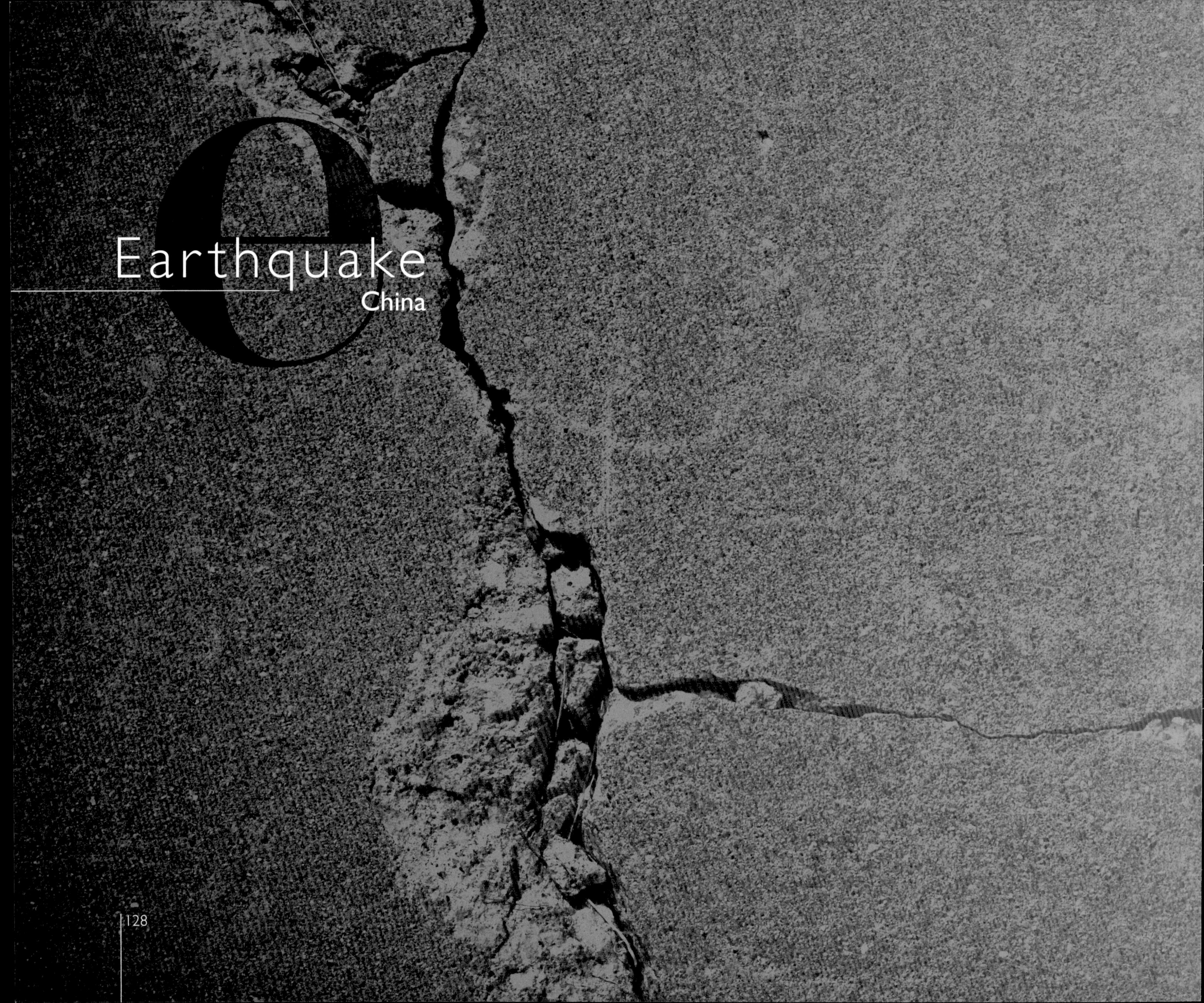

Earthquake

China

> "All of a sudden, the whole world was shaking. We were all swaying awfully… We heard some teachers yell, 'It's earthquake! Run! and then we all followed our teachers and ran out to the playground."
> Su Jie, aged 12

On 12 May 2008, China's Sichuan Province was hit by an earthquake measuring 8.0 on the Richter scale. The disaster killed more than 69,000 people and left more than 374,000 injured. Five million people in twelve separate districts were left homeless.

World Vision was able to mobilise staff and volunteers within hours to supply tarpaulins and tents as shelter, along with emergency supplies of quilts and bedding to tens of thousands of people.

Schools were reconvened in tents and prefabricated classrooms, with educational supplies including blackboards and sets of desks and chairs supplied by World Vision. Over 100 clinic tents provided temporary health centre services, while cooking utensils and solar heaters were given out to assist survivors with food and hot water. Child Friendly Spaces were set up to establish support for the emotional needs of children in shock from the disaster.

A key priority for the near future is helping to rebuild homes, schools and health clinics.

Earthquake
China

Yingxiu Township in Wenchuan County. This area of Sichuan was the most severely hit by the earthquake. Total devastation could be seen everywhere. Roads were broken, bridges torn apart and many buildings collapsed into debris.

Earthquake
China

Buildings crumbled to the ground in minutes as the earth shook.

e

Earthquake
China

A woman devastated by the loss of her home in the earthquake. She is being comforted by World Vision's Kevin Chiu while collecting a new quilt at a relief distribution centre.

Earthquake
China

Balconies buckled as the earthquake's force took hold. Until aftershocks subsided and structural damage could be assessed, residents risked their lives returning to their homes for shelter or emergency supplies.

The main street of Hongyan Township turned into a rubble-strewn ruin.

平安红岩
红岩镇

Earthquake
China

Broken roads and collapsed bridges in Yingxiu Township. Earthquake damage to infrastructure was acute throughout this part of Sichuan Province.

Earthquake
China

Food is distributed to survivors at one of many relief centres set up in the days following the disaster.

Earthquake
China

To keep children of this province engaged while their school days were suspended, World Vision distributed back to school and child friendly kits to boys and girls. Back to school kits contained items including a water bottle, stationery and a dictionary, while the child friendly kits for younger children contained simple toys and stickers.

Earthquake
China

Shenchai Primary School students now have lessons in tents, while survivors like 8-year-old Jin and her cousin are kept safe in a temporary refuge.

动 强 人 民

世界宣明會

Earthquake
China

Zhang lost two of his family members after the earthquake struck. Pictured here with artwork made at a Child Friendly Space session, Zhang, his friends and many other children will benefit from World Vision's earthquake rehabilitation program.

Earthquake
China

Liang Xing is working to rebuild his house and bring hope for the future to his family.

Global Food Crisis

Africa

Global Food Crisis

Africa

The developing world is facing a new kind of emergency: a food crisis that is gripping countries across the globe. Continuing droughts, devastating floods and other effects of climate change have combined with escalating food and fuel prices to push poor households, already struggling to afford basic foods, deeper into poverty. Children's nutrition, health, education and protection are all under threat.

This complex humanitarian disaster has the potential to halt the progress of years of development work, with millions of people across sub-Saharan Africa in urgent need of food right now.

Emergency food aid and supplementary feeding for malnourished children is being offered to meet the most immediate needs. Water and sanitation kits and seeds and tools are also being delivered. Communities are being trained in sustainable farming practices to create a more reliable supply of food and protect the fragile environment. World Vision is also working at a national and international level to reduce the impact of economic systems that disadvantage the world's poorest and most vulnerable.

> "From afar it may look hopeless, but once you get on the ground and see the context and the desire people have to live with dignity, you become sure that we can do it. It's possible, and we have demonstrated it."
> – Dr Hannibal Muhtar, World Vision

"I'm not so old that I have to sit and wait for food like a chicken. I can take care of things."
– Febby, farmer, mother and grandmother

Febby is part of World Vision's conservation farming program near Gwanda, Zimbabwe. The region has suffered for years from drought, leaving the land dry and inhospitable. "The greatest problem is hunger," she says. "The second is the disease that has taken the young people and left us behind with orphans."

Global Food Crisis
Africa

Agnes holds her 7-month-old daughter Jessica.

Agnes is a single mother with three children, living in Uganda. Agnes once grew the food she needed to survive on two acres of land, until rebel activity led her to flee for a relief camp. Now she earns her pay in food, but there is never enough quantity or quality for her family.

A child toils amid the parched landscape.

World Vision staff greet 120 people, mostly women, who are collecting food supplies in Zimbabwe's Gwanda District. The group at this distribution of bulgur wheat, vegetable oil and pinto beans are part of a conservation farming scheme. World Vision is working to ensure that more sustainable solutions to hunger and malnutrition are major priorities in the response to this crisis.

This lady is part of a farmers' association called *Tingania Ni Wutomi*, a community group of 47 members who work the land supported by World Vision. She is pictured here working alongside the group's chairman, Fernande.

The group provides jobs and lends and raises money to help members of their community, including those affected by HIV and AIDS. The crops they grow include onion, cabbage, carrots, tomatoes and sweet potatoes.

"This field has impact. [People] come here and work together and sing together and what they produce here is for their own health."
– Fernande, Chairman of *Tingania Ni Wutomi*

Claudine, 4, eats a plate of food at a distribution centre for malnourished children in southern Rwanda.

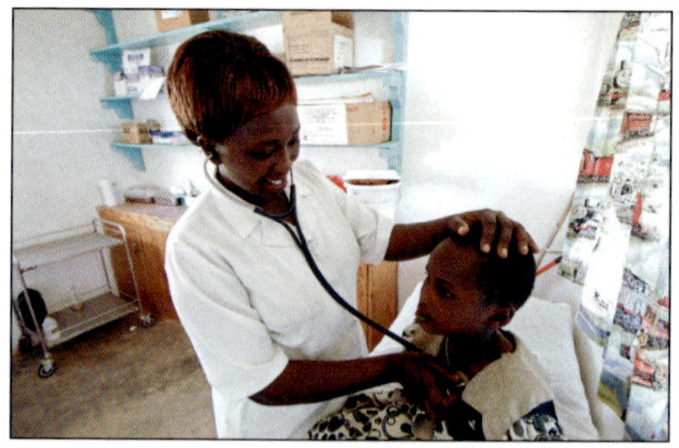

In this Kenyan clinic Doctor Joyce Mwangi checks on a child suffering from stomach complications, a common yet life-threatening complaint when nutritious food is scarce.

World Vision is working hard with communities in the Democratic Republic of Congo to ensure a steady supply of food is available for their children.

Moruengor, northern Kenya. Without this food distribution many people say they would perish.

World Vision
World Vision

This irrigation project started in 1996 when a dam was constructed in the Malole region of Zimbabwe. Now the scheme is being extended through food-for-work programs. Communities are creating trenches and a canal from the dam to the field. Workers are given food rations to last 30 days, including vegetable oil, cereals and beans.

Women work together to prepare land for plowing, with tools and seeds provided by World Vision.

Neo, aged 2, is given the last of the maize from yesterday's pot by his grandmother, Nkakole. World Vision provided food and other basic items to the family to prevent malnutrition and loss of life.

Salt water lake, the main water source for Mazamni village in Niger.

Acknowledgements

Photographic credits

Thank you to World Vision communicators, photographers and field staff around the world.

Tsunami
Page 34, 40, 54 - ADH/Stefan Trappe
Page 98 - Maida Irawani

Pakistan
Page 72, 74, 78, 86 - ADH/Stefan Trappe
Page 90 - ADH/Florian Kopp

Myanmar
Page 102, 109 - Names have been changed for protection reasons.
Page 106 - ADH/Loeffke

Thanks also to: Ashley Clements, Adele Glover, Lay Htoo, Suzy Sainovski, Alison Schafer, Martin Thiele, Madeleine Wilson.